Geisha Bookmarks

by Delores Frantz

Happy Geishas

MATERIALS: Craft sticks • ¾" round Woodsies • 5⅞" squares of origami paper • Black paper twist • Black and Red permanent pens • Tacky glue

The geisha... most fa... of Japan... and styliz... mind the Japanese love of beauty, tradition and the hundreds of years old tea ceremonies.

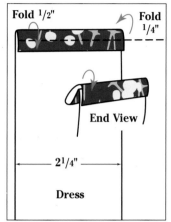

1. Fold 5⅞" x 2¼" origami paper down ½". Fold edge back the other way ¼".

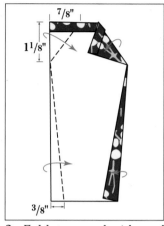

2. Fold top and sides of dress in as shown above.

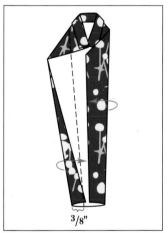

3. Fold sides in toward center again. Set aside.

4. Glue craftstick to woodsies and draw face.

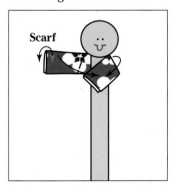

5. Cut out 1" x 2" scarf and fold in half. Glue to craftstick in back, fold each end to front and glue.

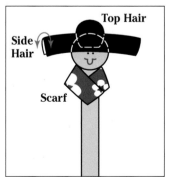

6. Cut out ¾" x 2" side hair and top hair from the paper twist. Fold the side hair in half. Place the woodsies head inside hair fold and glue. Glue the top

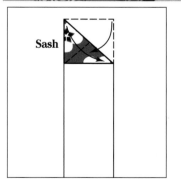

hair to the back of head. Fold the hair ends to the back and glue in place.

7. Fold 1⅛" x 3¾" sash as shown to form point at one end.

8. Put the dress on the craftstick and glue down the front. Glue sash to front of dress and fold right, then left sides to back. Glue. Cut out the hair ornaments and glue in place.

Fans & Umbrellas

by Nancy Taylor

It is believed that fan folding was invented in Japan about 700 AD. The fans were painted with bright colors and used in ceremonial dances.

It was not long until the Chinese began using fans. In 1500, the Portuguese brought fans to Europe where they were quickly accepted by women. Under Louis XV, men also carried fans.

Women have historically used fans as an aid in flirting and for acting coy.

1. Cut circle from paper. Stamp both sides Silver.

2. Fold paper in half, quarters and eighths, score.

3. Fold accordion style.

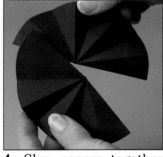

4. Glue papers together overlapping at center.

Blue Fan Card

MATERIALS: Hero Arts Chinese Seals, Tiny Icons and Flower Shadows rubber stamps • Blue patterned and silver origami papers • 12" of $\frac{1}{2}$" sheer blue ribbon • 12" of fine silver cord • Small silver tassels with cord • Silver stamp pad • $5\frac{1}{2}$" x 11" and $\frac{3}{4}$" x $1\frac{3}{8}$" pieces of white cardstock

INSTRUCTIONS: Fold 11" cardstock in half. Glue blue and silver paper as shown. Cut $4\frac{1}{2}$" circle from dark blue paper. Cut circle in half. Stamp both halves in silver and allow to dry. Score half circles into eighths. Fold accordion style. Glue half circles overlapping center edges. Attach to card with hot glue. Attach bows and tassels. Stamp tiny icon on $\frac{1}{2}$" blue square. Fold tiny tag and glue on blue square. Attach with cord.

Hint: Use extra postage and padded envelope for mailing this card.

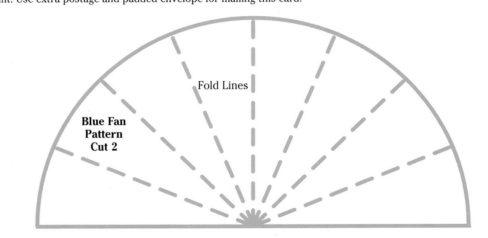

Fold Lines

Blue Fan Pattern Cut 2

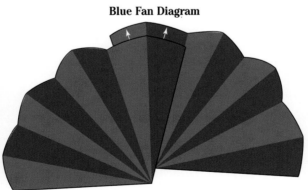

Blue Fan Diagram

Overlap and glue center edges of folded half circles to make one large fan. Glue to card.

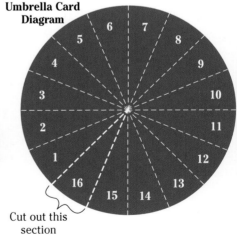

Umbrella Card Diagram

Cut out this section

Fan with Red Sash

MATERIALS: $6\frac{1}{2}$" x 10" ivory cardstock • 6" x 9" black cardstock • $5\frac{1}{2}$" x $8\frac{1}{2}$" yellow mulberry paper • 2" x 8" red vellum • 2" x $7\frac{1}{4}$" washi paper • Paper trimmer or scissors and ruler • Glue/adhesive

INSTRUCTIONS:
Fold ivory cardstock, black cardstock, yellow mulberry paper and red vellum in half. Slide red vellum over yellow mulberry paper over black cardstock over ivory cardstock. Secure each layer with a length of double-sided tape at back top fold between the layers. Fold fan following accordion fold diagram. Wrap small piece of washi paper around base of fan and glue. Spread fan and glue to center of card.

Umbrella Card

MATERIALS: Hero Arts Japanese Maiden, Bamboo with Leaves and Tiny Icons rubber stamps • Origami paper • Red cardstock • Square card and envelope • Gold stamp pad • 8" of $\frac{1}{4}$" red ribbon • 18" of fine gold cord • Tiny brass charms

INSTRUCTIONS: Cut origami paper and glue on card as shown. Cut $4\frac{1}{2}$" circle from paper and stamp gold, let dry. Score circle into sixteen sections. Cut one section away leaving 15 sections. Fold accordion style. Using a bamboo stick for handle, cover one end with matching paper and attach charms with gold cord. Attach bamboo and folded circle to card. Add bows and charms. Stamp tiny icon on $\frac{1}{2}$" red square. Fold tiny tag and glue on red square. Attach with cord.

Create charming cards with paper folded fans and umbrellas for every occasion.

Miniature Fans

Fan Notecard

MATERIALS: 3½" x 6" of black cardstock • 3 x 6" of gold paper • 2 x 4" of washi paper • 6" of gold cord • Double-sided tape

INSTRUCTIONS

Fold black cardstock in half. Fold gold cardstock in half. Slide gold card over black card. Secure with a length of double-sided tape at back top fold between layers. Fold washi paper into a fan following diagram. Wrap one end of accordion fold with gold cord and tie in a knot to secure. Spread fan to desired width and glue to front of card.

To Make Accordion Fold Miniature Fan

Start with a rectangle.

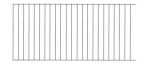

Draw guidelines on the back of folding paper.

1. To make pleats the same size and to fold accurately, lightly draw guidelines on the back of folding paper with a pencil and ruler. Draw guide marks every ³⁄₁₆" across the paper.

2. Fold paper back and forth creasing along each drawn line.

3. Shape accordion fold into a fan, stretching one end to desired fullness and tying off other end.

Fold paper back and forth creasing along each drawn line.

Add lace trim, a fancy tassel or bead trim for truly romantic fans!

Simply Fabulous Fans
with Beaded Tassels
by Jane Beard

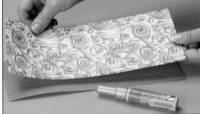

1. Glue printed paper on back of plain paper.

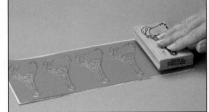

2. Stamp design down length of plain paper.

3. Emboss with heat tool.

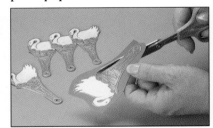

4. Cut out around stamped designs.

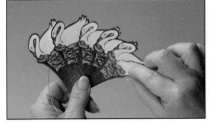

5. Punch holes and thread cord through blades.

6. Make tassel following instructions on page 33.

Framed Rose Fan

MATERIALS: 8" x 10" shadow box frame • Burgundy mat and forest green backing to fit frame • 4 large decorative beads, one large, one medium and 2 small • Gold bead caps • 2 hatpins
INSTRUCTIONS: Make fan and tassel. Secure mat and backing in frame. Glue fan to backing using small squares of foamboard to suspend fan above backing. Assemble hat pins and glue under fan as shown in photo.

Delicate Victorian Fans

MATERIALS: Museum of Modern Rubber Rose, Swan, Poinsettia, Heart Doily and Victorian Fan rubber stamps • Cardstock • Stamp pad • 1/8" ribbon or fine braided cord • Scissors • 1/8" hole punch • Embossing powder • Iridescent ink • Glitter • Markers • Fine metallic cord • 30 small glass beads

INSTRUCTIONS: Stamp each fan design 5 to 7 times. Emboss if desired. Color fan pieces. Cut out each fan blade. Punch a hole at the bottom of each blade. Cut 2 small slits in each blade or use hole punch. There are two guide marks on the stamp just below cluster of 3 small hearts. Thread ribbon or braided cord through bottom holes of all fan blades and tie. Lace a small length of ribbon or braided cord through each blade going from back to front. Adjust spacing of the blades and fasten ends of ribbon or cord to back with glue or tape.

Make tassels following instructions on page 33.

Spiritual Shrines

by Denise Jackson

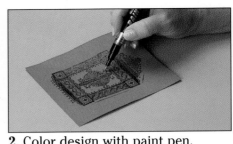

1. Stamp and emboss design for font of shrine.

2. Color design with paint pen.

3. Cut out and stamp back of shrine.

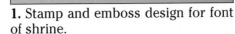

4. Use ruler and craft knife to cut door opening.

5. Fold doors.

6. Cover box with patterned paper.

7. Stamp and trim paper to fit box.

8. Make seal. Coil and attach wire.

9. Glue seal in center of box.

Yin Tzu Seal Shrine

MATERIALS: Uptown Design Shrine of the Divine, Letter from Abroad, Chinese Yin Tzu Seal and 2000 Year of the Dragon rubber stamps • Red cardstock • White paper • Small box, a cigarette box or small gift box • Black Colorbox™ ink pad • Clear embossing powder • Black Memories™ ink pad • Craft knife • Gold pen • Gold glitter spray • Mounting tape • Poly-Shrink plastic

INSTRUCTIONS:
Stamp the Shrine of the Divine on red cardstock with black Colorbox ink pad and emboss with clear powder. Color stars on top of shrine with gold pen and spray shrine with gold glitter. Cut out shrine and cut open doors with craft knife. Stamp the Yin Tzu Seal over and over on white paper with black Memories ink pad. Use to cover back and sides of box. Stamp Letter from Abroad on white paper with black Memories ink pad. Trim to fit and attach to inside of box. Stamp 2000 Year of the Dragon on polyshrink plastic with black Memories ink pad. Bake in a 300°F oven for 2 to 3 minutes. Cut 5 layers of foam tape to fit behind Dragon Symbol. Place curled pieces of wire between layers of foam tape. Attach Dragon Symbol inside shrine. Attach red shrine to the front of box.

Mini Matchbox Shrine

MATERIALS: Uptown Design Shrine of The Divine, Letter from Abroad, Japanese Artist Signature and Token #1 rubber stamps • White paper and cardstock • Black Memories™ ink pad • Gold leafing pen • Clear embossing powder • Small matchbox • Craft knife • Red brush marker

INSTRUCTIONS:
Stamp the Shrine of the Divine on white paper with black ink. Reduce 50% and copy onto white cardstock. Cut out mini shrine. Cut doors open with craft knife and draw a border around edges with gold leafing pen. Attach small jewels to shrine. Stamp Letter from Abroad on white cardstock with black ink. Cut and fold to cover a small matchbox. Stamp Japanese Artist Signature on white cardstock, trim to fit and tape inside matchbox. Add glitter glue around inside edges of drawer. Attach paper shrine on top of matchbox. Stamp Token #1 with black Memories ink pad on a small scrap of white cardstock and emboss with clear powder. Cut out token, color with red brush marker and attach inside shrine.

Silver Crane Shrine

MATERIALS: Uptown Design Shrine of the Divine, Letter from Abroad and Crane Etching rubber stamps • Black folded card • White cardstock • White Colorbox™ ink pad • Black Memories™ ink pad • Silver embossing powder • Craft knife • Mounting tape

INSTRUCTIONS:
Stamp Letter from Abroad on front of black folded card. Stamp Shrine of the Divine on separate piece of black cardstock with White Colorbox ink pad. Emboss shrine with silver powder and cut out. Cut doors open with craft knife. Stamp Crane Etching on white cardstock with black ink pad and emboss with clear powder. Attach shrine over Crane card. Attach shrine to front of card.

Many religions incorporate the use of shrines where the devout go on pilgrimages to give thanks, ask for favors or show devotion.
Some shrines are buildings of great beauty while others are small niches placed in a quiet corner of the home. Whether splendid or simple, each shrine is a focal point for religious devotion and an aid to spiritual harmony.

Gold Leafing

by Lynn Krucke

1. Stamp design on acetate with permanent ink, let dry.

2. Apply selected adhesive.

3. Carefully pat leaf on adhesive for desired look. Burnish with fingers or stiff bristle paintbrush.

4. Glue backing paper in place.

5. Cut out shape, add trim.

Basic Instructions for Leafing

MATERIALS: Acetate (8½" x 11" overhead transparencies) • Ink pad and permanent black ink • Solvent based stamp cleaner • Composition metallic leaf • Adhesive (Xyron machine or double stick sheets like Peel-n-Stick or a foiling glue that dries tacky and clear) • Stiff-bristle brush • Scissors
INSTRUCTIONS:
Shake permanent ink to mix thoroughly. Apply a small amount to blank pad. Spread ink on pad with nozzle of the ink bottle and allow time for the ink to soak into pad. Due to the fast-drying nature of these inks, they dry out quickly on pad. Add more ink to remoisten pad, and it can be used over and over. Ink selected stamps and stamp carefully onto acetate. Expect to practice a bit, because stamping on a non-porous surface such as acetate is tricky. Stamps have a tendency to slip. Leave plenty of room between images. Clean stamps immediately. Allow stamped images to dry completely. Trim around images leaving a border a little larger than needed for finished piece. You will give images a final trim later. Apply adhesive to stamped side. Note: this results in an image that will be reversed! If you have used a stamp with words, apply adhesive to the opposite side. Applying leaf to the same side as the stamped image leaves front totally smooth.
Applying Leaf - Carefully place flakes or sheets of leaf randomly onto the sticky surface pressing into place. Once image is entirely covered, use fingers or a stiff bristle brush to burnish leaf and remove excess. Save excess leaf. Trim image to final size and complete selected project.

Bamboo Card

MATERIALS: 4¼" x 5¼" sage green card • Stamp Francisco bamboo rubber stamp • 3¼" x 4½" brown and 2¾" x 4" green Exotic paper • Foam mounting tape • Stamp pad • ½" double-sided tape • Metallic leaf
INSTRUCTIONS: Stamp bamboo on acetate and apply leaf following basic instructions. Trim image to 2" x 3½" and set aside. Stamp bamboo repeatedly on front of card creating a tone-on-tone effect. Layer foiled bamboo image onto green exotic paper using foam mounting tape then add a layer of brown exotic paper. Attach to front of card as shown in photograph. Inside the card, place a strip of double sided tape along right edge. Remove protective paper and apply metallic flakes. Burnish with stiff brush or fingers to adhere leaf and remove excess. Trim away a small strip on the front of card to reveal this leafed edge.

Cherry Blossom Bookmark

FINISHED SIZE: 2" x 5½"
MATERIALS: Black cardstock • Hole punch • Corner rounder • Assorted yarns and fibers • Stamp Francisco Cherry Blossom rubber stamp
INSTRUCTIONS: Stamp cherry blossom image several times on acetate and apply leaf following basic instructions. Trim to desired size and attach to black cardstock cut to the same size. Punch hole at center top. Round corners. Cut 5 to 10 pieces of fiber 10" long, and tie through hole to finish bookmark.

Face Pin

FINISHED SIZE: 1½" x 1¾"
MATERIALS: Scrap of mat board • Stamp Francisco Face Postoid rubber stamp • Craft knife • Ruler • Cutting mat • Copper foiling tape • 1/16" hole punch • Jump rings • Head pins • Wire cutters • Round nose pliers • Assorted beads • Pin back • E6000
INSTRUCTIONS: Stamp face on acetate with permanent black ink and leaf following basic instructions. Mount piece on scrap of mat board and trim to desired size using craft knife and ruler. Remove protective backing from copper foil tape and apply to edge of piece in one continuous strip. Smooth tape down on front and back of pin. Punch 5 holes evenly spaced across bottom of pin with hole punch. Place beads on head pins in desired pattern. Trim head pins if they are too long and make a small loop at the top to secure beads. Thread each head pin onto a jump ring, and insert into a hole on the pin as shown. Close jump rings. Glue on pin back.

FeMail Art Card

MATERIALS: 4¼" x 5¼" Gold confetti cardstock • Stamp Francisco FeMail Art rubber stamps • ¼" x 6" strip of Black paper • Paper crimper • Tape or glue
INSTRUCTIONS: Stamp FeMail Art 3 times on acetate. Add leaf following basic instructions. Trim each image close to border and mount on a slightly larger piece of black cardstock. Set aside. Fold gold confetti cardstock in half. Stamp word stamp repeatedly on front of card to create background. Run black paper strip through paper crimper. Adhere strip to center of card. Attach leafed acetate images as shown to complete card.

These lovely gold leafed plants and people are reminiscent of the eco-art of Feng Shui which deals with conservation and ecology. Feng Shui tells us how to locate ourselves in the universe in a better way.

Perky Little Purses

by Denise Jackson

These purses are whimsical little caches where you can store tiny treasures. They make lovely gift boxes and will be as treasured as the gift!

1. Cut out purse and handle cover, stamp design.

2. Stamp the paper for purse flap.

3. Stamp and emboss the flap medallion.

4. Color medallion and glue on flap.

5. Fold purse pocket and glue in place.

6. Glue handle and handle cover on purse.

Purse Pocket Diagram

1. Fold 5" square diagonally. Unfold. Repeat from opposite corners. Unfold.

2. Turn paper over. Fold in half horizontally. Unfold.

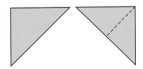

3. Turn paper over. Squash C & D to center to form triangles.

Your paper will look like this.

4. Fold A & B to center. Unfold. Repeat on other side.

5. Squash A & B to inside.

Chinese Flower Symbol Purse

MATERIALS: Uptown Design Chinese Flower Symbol and Letter from Abroad rubber stamps • Black Memories™ ink pad • White, Red and Yellow cardstock • Clear embossing powder • Red and Yellow brush markers • Red bead string • Mounting tape

INSTRUCTIONS: Trace purse pattern onto white cardstock and cut out. Stamp Chinese Flower Symbol on lower half of purse with black Memories ink. Attach red cardstock over top flap of purse. Stamp Letter from Abroad on red flap with black Memories ink. Stamp and emboss Chinese Flower Symbol with black Memories ink on a separate piece of white cardstock. Cut out center of image and attach over yellow cardstock. Trim yellow cardstock so that a small border of yellow shows. Attach image to red flap. Color a few areas with red and yellow brush markers. Attach red bead string to top for handle. Cut and fold a piece of yellow cardstock using purse pocket diagram and attach to inside of card.

Fold

Purse Handle Cover Pattern

Purse Pattern

Fold

Chinese Yin Tzu Seal Purse

MATERIALS: Uptown Design Chinese Yin Tzu Sea, Starflower Crest and Token #6 rubber stamps• Black cardstock • Embossing ink pad • Gold embossing powder • Gold spray glitter • Black bead string • Mounting tape

INSTRUCTIONS: Trace purse pattern onto cream cardstock and cut out. Cover outside of purse with black cardstock. Stamp Chinese Yin Tzu Seal on top flap and emboss with gold powder. Stamp Token #6 randomly all over bottom flap and emboss with gold powder. Spray bottom flap with gold spray glitter. Stamp Starflower Crest on a separate sheet of black cardstock and emboss with gold powder. Cut out Starflower and attach to flap. Attach black bead string for handle. Cut and fold a piece of cream cardstock using handle cover pattern and attach to inside of card.

Flowering Crest Purse

MATERIALS: Uptown Design Letter from Abroad, Token #1 and Flowering Crest rubber stamps • Black Memories™ ink • Gold Colorbox™ ink pad • Gold embossing powder • Red and Black cardstock • Poly-Shrink plastic • Red and Yellow brush markers • Mounting tape

INSTRUCTIONS: Trace purse pattern onto red cardstock and cut out. Stamp Letter from Abroad on bottom flap with black ink. Stamp Token #1 randomly with gold ink pad and emboss with gold powder. Attach black cardstock over top flap of purse. Stamp Letter from Abroad on black flap with gold ink pad and emboss with gold powder. Stamp Flowering Crest on poly-shrink plastic with black ink pad. Cut out crest and color with markers. Bake in a 300° oven for 2 to 3 minutes. Attach button to flap of purse with tape. Attach gold bead string for handle. Cut a piece of red cardstock using handle cover pattern and attach to inside of card.

Clever little coin holder and fortune holder purses have a surprise 'explosion' inside. Create a little purse in every color.

Images on Clay

by Lynn Krucke

Make your own artist style face accents. Use these unique creations for pendants, pins or box lids.

1. Stamp image firmly but gently on sheet of clay with black ink.

2. Trim image to desired shape and size.

3. Layer trimmed image on sheet of different color clay. Trim to make mat.

4. Curl rectangle of clay around skewer and press on back for bail.

Gold Face Pin

FINISHED SIZE: 2½" x 3"
MATERIALS: Stamp Francisco face rubber stamp • Black Memories™ ink
INSTRUCTIONS: Ink face stamp and stamp image onto sheet of gold clay. Trim and layer onto sheet of black clay. Trim black clay slightly larger than gold creating a mat for gold clay. Gently press with fingers or brayer to adhere pieces completely. Bake according to package directions. Coat with 2 coats of glaze or floor polish. Glue on pin back.

Bamboo Magnet

FINISHED SIZE: 2¼" x 1½"
MATERIALS: Gold Encore™ pigment ink • Stamp Francisco Bamboo rubber stamp
INSTRUCTIONS:
Use bamboo on gold clay for focal image. Ink bamboo stamp with gold ink and stamp black clay before adding gold clay layer. Glue magnet onto back of piece. Using same stamps and complimentary colors of cardstock, create a card to complement piece. A small piece of magnet glued onto card allows the finished piece to become a removable keepsake.

Red Stamped Box

FINISHED SIZE: 2½" x 3"
MATERIALS: Small papier mâché box • Red acrylic paint • Paintbrush or sponge • Gold Encore™ pigment ink • Gold leafing pen • Stamp Francisco Chung calligraphy and face rubber stamp
INSTRUCTIONS:
Paint box red, let dry. Ink calligraphy stamp with gold ink and stamp sides and top of box, let dry. Condition both colors of clay. Create focal clay piece following basic instructions, stamping image onto pearl clay and layer onto black clay. Adhere baked and glazed clay piece to top of box. Paint inside of box and rim of lid gold using leafing pen.

Basic Instructions for Clay

Note: Tools used for polymer clay should be dedicated to clay work and never used for food.
MATERIALS: Premo™ polymer clay (black, pearl, gold, silver) • Black Memories™ ink pad • Rolling pin or pasta machine • Rubber stamps • Craft knife or NuBlade™ • Polymer clay-friendly glaze or Future™ floor polish • Pin backs, magnets, or other findings as desired • E6000 glue, or 2-part epoxy glue
INSTRUCTIONS: Each of these projects uses 2 colors of Premo. The first is the surface to be stamped, the second frames the piece. Condition both colors of clay by rolling and squeezing until clay is soft and pliable or by rolling it several times through pasta machine at #1 setting. Fold between passes through machine. Using rolling pin or pasta machine, roll clay to be stamped into a sheet approximately ⅛" thick. Ink selected stamp with black Memories ink. Press stamp gently but firmly onto clay to transfer ink. Remove stamp. Trim clay to desired shape and size using craft knife or NuBlade. Set aside. Roll second clay color out to ⅛" thick sheet. Carefully place stamped clay piece onto this layer. Trim bottom layer so that it is slightly larger than top layer creating a mat for the stamped clay image. Gently press with fingers or brayer to be certain the layers are securely adhered. Take care not to distort stamped image. Bake following package directions. Remove from oven and allow to cool. Coat finished piece with glaze or floor polish. Attach pin back or magnet, or glue directly to project.

Silver Face Pin

FINISHED SIZE: 2" x 2¼"
MATERIALS: Toothpick • Plum Powdered Pearls • Stamp Francisco face rubber stamp
INSTRUCTIONS:
Stamp face onto silver clay and layer on black clay. To make border, roll a small rectangle of black clay the same thickness as the silver piece. Use toothpick to texture black clay with simple lines and scratches. With finger, lightly rub Powdered Pearls onto clay. Cut rectangle into small strips. Place strips around silver clay image, overlapping and trimming edges to create a frame. Once border is in place, trim black clay. Bake and finish, glue on pin back.

Black & Gold Pendant

FINISHED SIZE: 2½" x 3"
MATERIALS: Gold and Crimson Powdered Pearls • Soft bristle paintbrush • Wood skewer • Rubber Poet face stamp
INSTRUCTIONS:
Roll black clay into ⅛" thick sheet. Using finger or paintbrush, apply gold and crimson Powdered Pearls over the entire surface of clay. Ink stamp, stamp clay and trim. Complete piece following basic instructions. Once piece is baked, create a bail on the back for the pendant's cord or chain by rolling out a small rectangle of gold clay a little less than ⅛" thick. Place skewer or handle of paintbrush in center of rectangle and bring ends together to make a loop. The skewer helps hold loop open. Adhere bail to back of finished piece smoothing ends to blend edges into pendant. Rebake piece. Once cool, add chain or cord to complete pendant.
Note: It is possible to add this bail before baking the piece the first time, but it is more difficult to adhere bail well without distorting image.

Spectacular faces and portraits grace the cover of a box, the front of a card, or make stunning pendants and pins. Stamp them on oven-bake clay or on paper.

Chinese Take-Out
by Mary O'Neil

1. Glue papers together, fold.

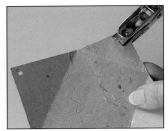

2. Punch holes in corners.

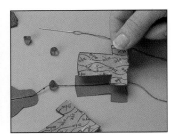

3. Stamp kimono and lantern designs on papers.

4. Glue designs together sandwiching thread.

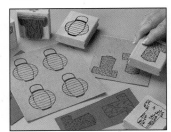

5. Tie thread hangers to the top piece.

6. Glue trim on top piece.

Chinese Take-Out Folding Pattern

Fold / Fold / Fold / Fold

Chinese Take-Out

MATERIALS: Hot Potatoes® Baby Quasi Mono, Little Miss Dragonfly and Baby Light My Flier rubber stamps • Chinese to-go box • Black ink pad • Red, Yellow and Black cardstock • 4 amber colored beads • Black embroidery thread • Beading needle • Paper adhesive • Scissors • Hole punch • Bone folder

INSTRUCTIONS:
Measure opening of to-go box. In this case opening is $2\frac{1}{2}$" x $3\frac{1}{2}$". Cut yellow and black rectangles, glue together. Using halfway mark as a starting point, measure down $2\frac{1}{2}$" on 2 longer sides of rectangle. Make lines long enough so that lines intersect. These will become the hanging points on the boxes. Fold using bone folder. Punch a small hole near end of each point. Stamp Little Miss Dragonfly 2 times on red cardstock and 2 times on yellow. Stamp Little Quasi Mono 2 times on Yellow cardstock and 2 times on red. Stamp Baby Light My Flier 8 times on yellow cardstock. Cut out all images. Using 12" of doubled thread, glue a red and yellow lantern on end sandwiching thread. Tie a knot and thread on a bead. Glue a red and yellow kimono above bead. Tie end of thread through hole in top piece. Repeat 3 more times. Cut a $2\frac{1}{2}$" square of red paper and fold in fourths. Glue on top for hanger.

Kimono Wash Line Card

1. Stamp and cut out kimonos.

2. Fold down tabs and glue kimonos to thread.

3. Punch holes in card, insert thread and tie knot.

4. Glue trim papers on card covering knot.

Kimono Wash Line Card

MATERIALS: Hot Potatoes® Bamboo, Little Miss Dragonfly, Baby Yoko Mono, Baby Haiki-Mono, Baby Quasi-Mono, Black Dragonfly, Love and Open Dragonfly rubber stamps • Handmade or Mulberry paper in green, red, white, black and beige • Grey cardstock • 8" piece of string • Scissors • Black and Sepia ink pad • Adhesive

INSTRUCTIONS:
Using gray cardstock, make 5" square card. Stamp with bamboo using black and sepia ink. Tear a piece of black mulberry paper to fit over one half of card. Wet your finger and rub it along the area to be torn for a lovely edge. Tear a piece of red paper approximately $2\frac{1}{2}$" x $3\frac{1}{2}$". Stamp Love on red paper with black ink. Stamp one kimono on each of the mulberry papers using black ink. Cut out each kimono leaving a paper doll clothes tabs. Stamp inside of the card using sepia ink and bamboo and dragonfly stamps. Place kimonos so they hang over string and glue tabs down. Make 2 small holes in card and run clothesline through each hole making a small knot to secure line. Glue black paper and then Red paper on front of card.

Create a darling 'Pull-Up' chinese take-out
box full of symbols and goodies. Or make
a kimono clothesline inside of a card.

Terrific Tags

by Lynn Krucke

Let's play tag! These projects demonstrate the versatility of tags… the ideas and uses for them are nearly unlimited! They are inexpensive, come in a variety of shapes and sizes, and are readily available.

Mini Notepad. With decorated side up, score along fold lines.

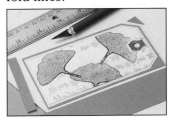

Tag Card. Trim each layer following the shape of the tag to give the card a unique look.

Memory Book. Add decorative fibers to tags.

Purse. Insert gussets on each side of tag matching edges. Fold down top.

Spiral-Bound Tag Book. With skewer held beside book, loop wire through holes to make spiral binding. Add beads if desired.

Mini Notepad
SIZE: 2¾" x 4¾"
MATERIALS: Stamp Francisco rubber stamps • Decorated tag • Scoring tool • Ruler • Bone folder • Stapler • Mini restickable note pad • Double-sided tape • Optional for necklace: ⅛" hole punch • Eyelet and setting tool • Satin cord
INSTRUCTIONS:
Decorate tags as desired. Fold at scores, creasing well. Staple flap to secure. If you are making a pendant, punch a hole in the center of tag between middle scores and install an eyelet to reinforce the hole. Add satin cord or ribbon to create necklace. Use double sided tape to add notepad. Fold over top and tuck into bottom flap to close pad.

Tag Card
SIZE: 2¾" x 4¾"
MATERIALS: Stamp Francisco rubber stamps • Decorated tag • Cardstock scraps in 2 shades of green • 3" x 11" of dark green cardstock • Glue or double-sided tape • Metallic embroidery floss • Scissors or paper cutter
INSTRUCTIONS:
Fold dark green cardstock in half to create card 3" x 5½" inches tall. Layer decorated tag onto cardstock scraps. Trim corners of each to mimic the shape of the tag. Adhere these layers to dark green card trimming corners the card as well. Tie metallic embroidery floss through the hole on the tag for embellishment.

Memory Book
SIZE: 2¾" x 4¾"
MATERIALS: Stamp Francisco rubber stamps • Decorated tags • Photographs • Scissors • Adhesive • Binder ring • Assorted fibers and ribbons
INSTRUCTIONS:
Glue photos on tags. Tie fibers and ribbons through hole in each tag. Thread tags on binder ring.

Purse-Pendant
SIZE: 3¼" x 6¼"
MATERIALS: Tag • Fabric • Xyron™ machine or spray adhesive • Templates • Scoring tool • Ruler • Strong but flexible paper for gussets • Glue or narrow double-sided tape • Tapestry needle • Jump rings • Small piece of hook and loop tape • Hole punch • Assorted fibers • Satin cord
INSTRUCTIONS:
Score tag following diagram. Cover tag with fabric. Use the Xyron machine or coat the tag with spray adhesive then add fabric. Trim away any excess. Fold covered tag on the scored lines to create basic shape of purse. Cut 2 gussets from strong, flexible paper. You may wish to color these pieces in a matching or a contrasting color. Fold on indicated lines, and apply glue or tape to all 3 flaps on each gusset. Insert one on each side of the tag matching the edges carefully. Punch hole in fabric where it covers existing hole in tag. Add selected fibers to embellish closure. With tapestry needle, make small holes on each side of flap to insert jump rings. Thread cord through jump rings and under flap to create necklace. Add small piece of hook and loop tape under flap to hold purse closed.

Spiral Bound Book
SIZE: 1½" x 2¾"
MATERIALS: Stamp Francisco rubber stamps • ¹⁄₁₆" hole punch • 24 gauge wire • Wire cutters • Round nose pliers • Beads • Wood skewer • Assorted ribbons or fibers • Charms and beads
INSTRUCTIONS:
Decorate several small tags to create pages for the book. Punch small holes, evenly spaced, along the left side of each page. Make sure the holes will line up when the book is assembled. Pull a length of wire through the top hole, from back to front. Place the skewer alongside the book and loop wire around it and through each hole. Pull wire tight to form even, round, loops on spiral binding. If desired, add a bead to wire at every loop. Once the binding is complete, cut excess wire and use pliers to create small loops or spirals at each end to secure binding. Add ribbon accent to binding, and tie small charms through reinforced hole on each page with selected fibers.

Purse Pattern

Fold

Mini-Notebook Pattern

Fold

Fold

Fold

Purse Gusset Pattern

Fold

*Tags are the perfect way
to showcase favorite photos.*

*Any photograph can be trimmed and used, but the Polaroid I-Zone™
camera takes tiny photos with no cropping required! The binder ring
opens and closes easily and fastens securely. The order of the pages
can be rearranged. Girls of all ages will enjoy the tiny purse. It is
roomy enough for a few tiny treasures. The secret is the gusseted sides.*

Tea Bag Stars

by Lani Temple

Add the art of tea bag folding to greeting and note cards. Gather your supplies and begin folding today. The results are guaranteed to be colorfully spectacular!

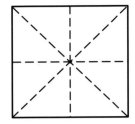

1. Start with white side of paper up. Fold each square diagonally both ways, then in half both ways; unfold.

2. Fold the top corner down to make a triangle.

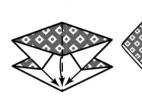

3. Push left and right corners inward making two reverse folds... bringing the top down so all four corners meet at the bottom, forming a diamond.

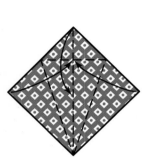

4. Fold both side points of the upper layer to the center; unfold. Fold the top down; unfold.

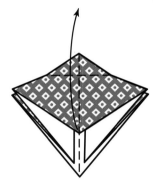

5. Separate the top layer and pull the bottom point up, the side points will pull in to center and meet.

6. Flatten the sides to form a long narrow diamond. Note: A small triangle will form under the diamond.

7. Interlock: Slip the left point of the bottom layer of one piece under the top layer of another. Repeat with all eight folded diamonds. Dot glue in folds to secure.

This special star fold fits inside of a cut-out circle. It can be viewed from BOTH the inside and the outside of a card.

Red & Black Star Card

MATERIALS: 6½" x 11" red cardstock • 5½" x 6½" black cardstock • 4" x 8" piece of of red vellum • Asian Fan rubber stamp • Black ink pad • Chinese coin • 6" Black wire • Paper trimmer or scissors and ruler • Glue/adhesive
INSTRUCTIONS:
Fold red cardstock in half. Rubber stamp fan design all over red vellum. Cut red vellum into 2" x 2" squares. Fold squares following tea-bag folding diagram. Glue together. Glue to black cardstock. Trim black cardstock ½" larger than tea-bag fold span. Wrap wire around Chinese coin. Make a small hole in center of tea-bag fold, insert ends of wire and twist to secure on back side.

Red & Gold Star

MATERIALS: 5½" x 11" of Black cardstock • 5" x 5" Gold vellum • 4½" x 4½" of Red vellum • Eight 2" squares of red washi paper • Circle cutter • Paper trimmer or scissors and ruler • Glue/adhesive • Double-sided tape
INSTRUCTIONS:
Fold black cardstock in half. Glue red and gold vellum on black cardstock. Fold tea-bag fold from washi paper following tea-bag folding diagram. With a toothpick, dab glue between each piece to secure in star shape. Using a circle cutter, cut a circle in center of red, gold and black card fronts.

Outside of the card.

Inside of the card.

Green & Black Card

MATERIALS: 5½" x 11" of black cardstock • 4½" x 10" of green vellum • Eight 2" squares of black washi paper • 12" of gold cord • Circle cutter • Paper trimmer or scissors and ruler • Glue/adhesive • Double-sided tape

INSTRUCTIONS:

Fold black cardstock and green vellum in half. Slide green vellum over black cardstock. Secure with a length of double-sided tape at back top fold between the layers. Fold tea-bag fold from washi paper following diagram. With a toothpick, dab glue between each piece to secure star shape. Using a circle cutter, cut a circle in center of green and black card fronts. Slide folded star inside cut circle. Tie gold cord around fold of card.

Flared Kimonos

by Lani Temple

Kimonos are the traditional dress of Japan. Usually Western clothes are worn to work while the kimono is favored at home. Worn by both men and women, the kimono is a long robe tied with an elaborate sash. The kimono is always worn for holidays and special occasions.

Kimonos

MATERIALS: Assorted 2" x 8" pieces of patterned paper • Glue/adhesive
INSTRUCTIONS:
Fold each kimono following folding diagram. Start with a rectangle.

1. Fold a small cuff at bottom of paper. Turn over.

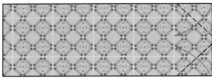

2. Fold right corner up to almost center. Repeat on left

3. Fold bottom up leaving 2".

4. Fold top down just above bottom crease.

5. Fold right top corner just past center diagonally. Repeat on left side.

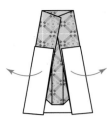

6. Fold top layer of bottom right, out to lie flat. Repeat on left side.

7. Fold top right corner out diagonally. Repeat on left side.

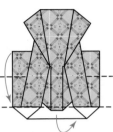

8. Fold bottom edge backward behind collar of kimono. Fold top edge of back layer back towards bottom.

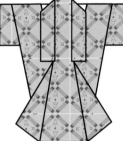

9. Turn over and bring collar to outside.

Kimono Cards

by Lani Temple

Kimono Cards

PHOTO ON PAGE 24
MATERIALS: Assorted 2" x 8" pieces of patterned paper • 5½" x 11" black cardstock • 4", 4½" and 5" pieces of patterned paper or vellum • Glue/adhesive
INSTRUCTIONS:
For each card, fold cardstock in half. Glue patterned papers and vellum to front of card as desired. Fold one or 2 kimonos following folding diagram and glue to front of each card. Tie cord or ribbon around waist of kimono if desired.

Large Kimono Card

MATERIALS: 6½" x 10" gold cardstock • 4½" x 6" black cardstock • 2" x 8" washi paper • 6" of orange ribbon • Two ¼" x 2" washi paper strips • Paper trimmer or scissors and ruler • Glue/adhesive
INSTRUCTIONS:
Fold gold cardstock in half. Glue black cardstock to center of gold cardstock. Fold washi paper following kimono folding diagram. Tie orange ribbon around waist of kimono. Glue kimono to center of card with back of kimono showing. Glue 2 small strips of washi paper to right and left side of card.

Small Kimono Card

MATERIALS: 3½" x 8½" gold cardstock • 2½" x 7" burgundy mulberry paper • 2" x 8" washi paper • 6" of gold cord • Paper trimmer or scissors and ruler • Glue/adhesive • Double-sided tape
INSTRUCTIONS:
Fold gold card in half. Fold mulberry paper in half. Slide mulberry paper over gold cardstock. Secure with a length of double-sided tape at back top fold between the layers. Fold kimono following folding diagram. Tie gold cord around waist. Glue to front of card.

Add oriental style and Japanese grace to your cards with bright and cheerful kimonos.

continued on page 24

Kimono Cards

Instructions on page 22.

Add oriental style and Japanese grace to your cards with bright and cheerful kimonos.

There are Celtic symbols for the various spiritual conditions of mankind. Celtic 'Knotwork Patterns' represent the journey of life and an attempt to understand the maze of our existence.

Celtic Hangers

by Lori Bodnar

1. Emboss the design using the stencil.

2. Color the embossed design area.

3. Glue the design on the colored paper.

4. Glue the designs together sandwiching cord.

5. Add assorted beads to the ends of cord.

MATERIALS: Two 8½" x 11" sheets of white cardstock • Two 8½" x 11" sheets of red cardstock • Black quilter's thread • Assorted beads to match colored cardstock • Pigmented ink pad • Dreamweaver Celtic Knot LL326, LM180, LM178 and LM160 stencils • Embossing tool or stylus • Light box • Scissors or craft knife • Metal ruler • ¼" stencil brush • Fine sewing needle • Glue stick

INSTRUCTIONS:
Cut white cardstock into two 3" x 3" pieces, two 2¼" x 2¼" pieces, two 3¼" circles, and two 3½" equilateral triangles. Dry emboss LL326 onto 3" x 3" pieces, LM178 onto 2¼" x 2¼" pieces, LM160 onto 3¼" pieces and LM180 onto the 3½" triangles. Using stencil brush and pigmented ink pad, stencil onto designs by repositioning appropriate stencil over each design. Cut red cardstock into two 3¼" x 3¼" pieces, two 2½" x 2½" pieces, two 3½" circles and two 3¾" triangles. Use glue stick to glue each white design to corresponding red piece. Cut 45" piece of thread, thread needle and knot end. Choose a bead for dangle at bottom of mobile. Thread it first and follow with 5 to 7 other beads. Place LM178 design face down and apply glue stick to entire back side. Tightly stretch thread through center from bottom to top. Apply second LM178 design face up and press to secure all edges. Thread on 7 more beads and repeat using LL326 design, then LM180 design and finally LM160 design. At top, continue with small size beads for 3". Loop back to first beads at top, thread back through 3 beads and tie off. Snip off the extra thread. Hang mobile and allow it to dry for 15 minutes.

Create a beautiful hanging mobile.

Happi Coats

by Lani Temple

Craft a sense of whimsical fun with these little three-dimensional garments made from washi paper. Attach them to handmade cards for added fun.

MATERIALS: 4" x 4" pieces washi paper for Happi coat and Yakko • Paper trimmer or scissors and ruler • Glue/adhesive
INSTRUCTIONS:
Fold washi paper according to Happi coat fold diagrams and Yakko fold diagrams

Gold, Black & Red Card - Happi Coat and Yakko

MATERIALS: 6½" x 10" gold cardstock • 4½" x 6" black cardstock • 4¼" x 5½" yellow mulberry paper • 2½" x 3" red vellum • Two 4" x 4" pieces washi paper for Happi coat and Yakko • Paper trimmer or scissors and ruler • Glue/adhesive
INSTRUCTIONS:
Fold gold cardstock in half. Glue black cardstock to gold cardstock. Glue yellow mulberry paper to black cardstock. Glue red vellum to center of yellow mulberry paper. Fold washi paper according to Happi coat fold diagram and Yakko fold diagram. Glue Happi coat and shawl to right and left front of card, just off center and diagonal to one another.

Gold & Black Card - Happi Coat and Yakko

MATERIALS: 6½" x 10" Black cardstock • 6" x 9½" gold cardstock • Two 4" x 4" pieces washi paper for Happi coat and Yakko • Paper trimmer or scissors and ruler • Glue/adhesive • Double-sided tape
INSTRUCTIONS:
Fold black cardstock in half. Fold gold cardstock in half. Slide gold over black cardstock. Secure with a length of double-sided tape at back top fold between the layers. Fold washi paper according to Happi coat fold diagram and Yakko fold diagram. Glue Happi coat and shawl to right and left front of card just off center and diagonal to one another.

Traditional Happi Coat: Start with a square.

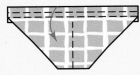 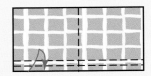 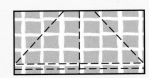 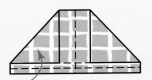 

1. Fold paper in half vertically, unfold. Fold in half horizontally.

2. Fold up bottom cuff, unfold.

3. Fold corners diagonally.

4. Fold bottom cuff up.

5. Turn over and upside down.

6. Fold top cuff down.

7. Fold corners down diagonally.

8. Your folded paper will look like this. Turn over.

9. Pull center fold up and out as shown.

10. Your folded paper will look like this. Turn over.

11. Your Happi Coat will look like this.

Traditional Yakko Fold: Start with a square.

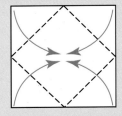     

1. Fold each corner in to center point. Turn paper over.

2. Again, fold each corner in to center point. Turn over.

3. Your paper will look like this. Turn over.

4. Your folded paper will look like this.

5. Fold each corner to center point. Turn over.

6. Your paper will look like this

7. Squash 3 corners out.

8. Your paper will look like this while squashing.

9. Your finished Yakko fold will look like this.

Mini Book

by Lynn Krucke

Mini Book

FINISHED SIZE: 1¼" x 1½"

MATERIALS: Paper Parachute black text weight paper • Small scrap of cardstock • Stamp Francisco face postoid rubber stamp • ¹/₁₆" hole punch • 22 gauge wire • Wire cutters • Wood skewer • Round nose pliers • Assorted small beads • Assorted fibers • Satin cord

INSTRUCTIONS: Stamp face on acetate with permanent black ink and leaf according to general instructions. Trim acetate to 1¼" x 1½" Cut a small piece of cardstock and several pieces of black paper to the same size. Punch holes across the top of each piece matching them to be sure holes are even. Coil wire around a wood skewer. Holding all pages together, thread wound wire through punched holes. Make an extra loop on each end for the satin cord to pass through when the pendant is strung. Tie fibers threaded with beads to wire as shown.

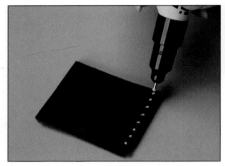

1. Mark covers and punch holes.

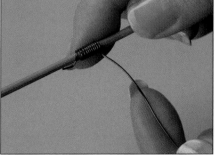

2. Coil wire around wood skewer.

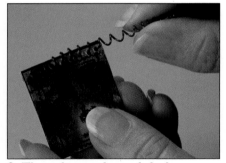

3. Thread wire through holes.

Inside of the Memo Book and Mini-Book.

Lantern Memo Book

by Lynn Krucke

Memo Book

FINISHED SIZE: 3¼" square

MATERIALS: Stamp Francisco Lantern and Chinese Character rubber stamps • Small book of your choice, purchased or handcrafted • Mizuhiki cord • Wood skewer • Glue gun and glue sticks • Clear embossing ink • Crimson Powdered Pearls • Acetate sheet • Gold leaf

INSTRUCTIONS: Stamp lantern on acetate and apply leaf according to general instructions on page 10. Trim image to 2" x 2½" and mount on front of small book. Ink Chinese character stamp with clear embossing ink and set aside. Twist each of three 12" lengths of mizuhiki cord tightly around skewer until they hold a spiral shape when released. Find the middle of each and gently shape them into L shapes. Use the glue gun to apply a blob of glue to the upper left corner of the image, holding the mizuhiki cords in place so that they will be adhered with the glue. Gently place the stamp you inked earlier with clear ink into the glue. Do not press it in hard! Be patient! Wait for the glue to cool completely before removing the stamp. With your finger, rub a bit of the crimson Powdered Pearls over the glue seal to highlight the stamped image.

1. Cover mat board with Black paper.

2. Glue spine paper on cover to reinforce.

Outside of the Memo Book and Mini-Book.

Everyone loves little books... and these are made extra special with metallic inks and gold leafing.

3. Glue lining paper in place.

4. Glue Post-it notes inside the cover.

5. Add design and cord to front cover.

Harmony is the state of being where all of life's conditions are in balance. The Chinese believe that all life and nature should be tn harmony to create a sense of unity.

Accordion Booklet

by Nancy Taylor

Accordion books are full of surprises. Each page is filled with a new view or message.

1. Stamp and color the designs.

2. Glue black and stamped paper on cardboard.

3. Stamp hinges.

4. Glue hinges between front and back pieces.

5. Glue cord loop between top front and back pieces.

Accordion Booklet

MATERIALS: Hero Arts Asian Swirl Fan, Japanese Maiden, Bamboo with Leaves, Seals and Ornamental Borders rubber stamps • Watercolor pencils • Black and white paper • Cardboard • Gold ink pad • Black rattail • Black permanent marker • Black button
INSTRUCTIONS: Cut 4 pieces of cardboard $3\frac{1}{2}$" x 3". Use black marker to color edges of all cardboard pieces. Stamp images in black on white paper. Color as desired. Cut three $1\frac{3}{4}$" x $2\frac{1}{2}$" pieces of black paper and stamp in gold. Cut eight $3\frac{1}{2}$" x 3" pieces of black paper. Mount images on black paper and glue to cardboard. Mount hinge pieces between black backing paper and cardboard as shown. Attach loop between cardboard and black paper at one end and a button or tie at the other end.

Heart Fold Card

by Lani Temple

Red & Gold Heart

MATERIALS: $6\frac{1}{2}$" x 10" Ivory cardstock • 4" x $5\frac{1}{2}$" red mulberry paper • 3" x 3" Gold cardstock • 2" x 6" red washi paper • Paper trimmer or scissors and ruler • Glue/adhesive
INSTRUCTIONS:
Fold ivory cardstock in half. Glue red mulberry paper to center of ivory cardstock. Glue gold cardstock to center of red mulberry paper. Fold washi paper according to heart fold diagram. Glue to center of card.

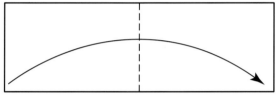

1. Fold in half.

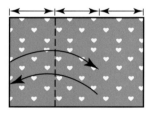

2. Fold $\frac{1}{3}$ of width, unfold.

3. Unfold again to leave a single layer on right side.

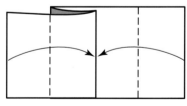

4. Fold each side into center.

5. Fold each corner into fold, unfold.

  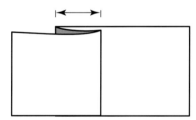 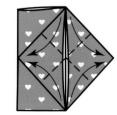 

6. Squash open each corner into center fold.

7. Fold each center corner diagonally to meet side corners.

8. Squash open center folds to meet in center.

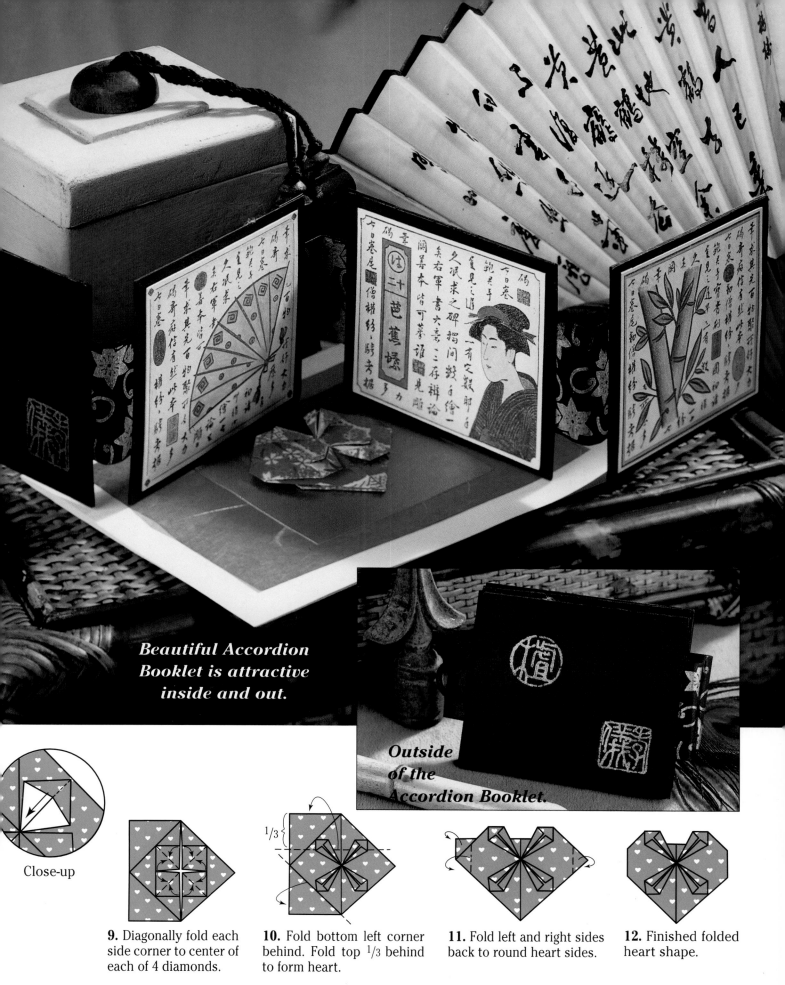

Beautiful Accordion Booklet is attractive inside and out.

Outside of the Accordion Booklet.

Close-up

1/3

9. Diagonally fold each side corner to center of each of 4 diamonds.

10. Fold bottom left corner behind. Fold top 1/3 behind to form heart.

11. Fold left and right sides back to round heart sides.

12. Finished folded heart shape.

Create a 5-minute beaded pen to add beauty to your everyday writing chores. What a wonderful way to bring harmony and joy to your day.

Treasure Beadz Pens with Tassels

by Diane Ferree

MATERIALS: Treasure Beadz™ • Micro Beedz • 1" Terrifically Tacky Tape™ • Bic or Papermate stick pen
INSTRUCTIONS:
Cut a length of tape equal to length of pen, leaving tip uncovered and about ¼" extra at end. Place pen on the lengthwise center of tape. Starting ½" above top, wrap tape around pen. Peel off liner, fold down extra at top. Roll in Beedz. If you are using Treasure Beadz, start with them and carefully press all bugle beadz flat. Make sure that there are no large empty spaces. Then roll pen in micro Beedz. Scrunch micro Beedz in with your fingers to make sure all holes are filled.

1. Place pen flat on tape and cut tape ¼" past end.

2. Wrap tape around pen, loosen liner and overlap tape slightly. Peel off liner and wrap end of tape over end of pen.

3. Roll pen in Treasure Beadz. Press down firmly. Do not leave uneven beads sticking out.

4. Roll pen in micro Beedz.

Square Patch Card

by Nancy Taylor

1. Glue square patches on card.

2. Tie raffia around twig.

MATERIALS: Hero Arts Little Greetings Many Thanks rubber stamp • Square card and Envelope • Origami papers
INSTRUCTIONS: Cut twelve ¾" squares from washi type paper. Stamp Thanks at bottom. Glue squares on white card. Glue Bamboo and red raffia on top.

3. Glue twig on card.

Beautiful Beaded Tassels

Beaded tassels are always in style. Attach them to the Fabulous Fans shown on pages 6 & 7 or just about anything else around the house. They are great for ceiling fans, door knobs, lamps, china cabinets or even decorative pillows. The possibilities are never ending.

by Mary Libby Neiman

Tassel on a fan... from pages 6-7.

Tassels are shown smaller than actual size.

1. Thread 100 bead on 10 yards of doubled 2-ply metallic thread.

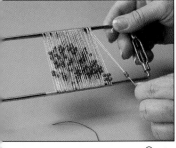

2. Wind around Tatool® 50 times leaving 2 beads on each turn.

3. Cut 15" of doubled thread, wrap around top of tassel with hangman's knot. Spin 16" rope.

4. Shorten tool by turning adjusters clockwise. Pull rope through and slide bottom of tassel off bottom of tool. Lengthen tool until adjusters are released completely. Slide top of tassel off tool.

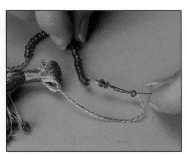

5. Thread 30 beads on rope and tie into 3 groups of 5 on each side.

Create lovely accessories to grace any wedding... place card, napkin ring and invitation.